D1571756

OTHER HELEN EXLEY GIFTBOOKS IN THIS SERIES:

A Feast of After Dinner Jokes
A Portfolio of Business Jokes
A Megabyte of Computer Jokes
A Century of Cricket Jokes
A Bouquet of Wedding Jokes
A Round of Golf Jokes

Over 30s' Jokes
A Spread of Over 40s' Jokes
A Triumph of Over 50s' Jokes
A Jubilee of Over 60s' Jokes
Old Wrecks' Jokes
A Knockout of Sports Jokes

If you've enjoyed this joke book, then try *A Chuckle of Kids Jokes*,
also published by Exley.

Published simultaneously in 2000 by Exley Publications Ltd in Great Britain,
and Exley Publications LLC in the USA.

12   11   10   9   8   7   6   5   4   3   2   1

Cartoons © Bill Stott 2000
Copyright © Helen Exley 2000
The moral right of the authors has been asserted.

ISBN 1-86187-126-0

Series Editor: Helen Exley
Editor: Claire Lipscomb

Printed and bound in Hungary.

Exley Publications Ltd, 16 Chalk Hill, Watford, Herts WD1 4BN, UK.
Exley Publications LLC, 232 Madison Avenue, Suite 1409, NY 10016, USA.

Crazy Kids' Jokes

A HELEN EXLEY GIFTBOOK

≣EXLEY
NEW YORK • WATFORD, UK

Jumbo Jokes

How can you tell if there's an elephant in your refrigerator?
Footprints in the butter.
How do you get two elephants in your refrigerator?
Buy more butter.

Why does the light in your refrigerator go out when you close the door?
The elephant turns it off.

Why couldn't the elephant fit through the keyhole?
He had a knot in his tail.

What has a long trunk, big ears and is found in Iceland?
A lost elephant.

How do you get an elephant in a
telephone booth?
Open the door.

What did Tarzan say when he saw a herd of
elephants on the horizon?
"Look! A herd of elephants on the horizon."
What did Tarzan say when he saw a herd
of elephants wearing dark glasses, on
the horizon?
Nothing. He didn't recognize them.
What did Tarzan say when he
saw a herd of zebras
on the horizon?
"Ha! You elephants
can't fool me again
with your disguises!"

Spider Soup

Waiter! Why is there a spider in my soup?
To catch the flies, Madam.

DINER: Waiter! What's that snail doing on my lettuce?
WAITER: About half a mile, Sir.

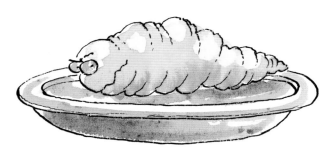

Waiter, waiter, there are maggots in
this pie.
Ssh, Sir, or they'll all be wanting some.

Waiter, waiter, there's a beetle in my stew!
Such honesty! I'll add it to your tab.

Waiter, waiter, there's a fly in my
soup.
Don't worry, Madam. It's wiped its
feet on your napkin.

Revolting Relatives

MOTHER: Tina! Why have you put a slug in your brother's bed?
TINA: Because I couldn't find a rat.

DAD: Have you put on a new pair of socks each morning this week?
CHILD: Yes, and I can't get my shoes on.

LITTLE GIRL: Our pet snake is just like one of the family.
LITTLE BOY: Really, which one?

FATHER: Have you brushed your teeth? Everyone can see you had toast for breakfast!
SON: No, I had toast yesterday.

DAD: Why has the teacher sent you home early today?
KID: Because the boy next to me was smoking.
DAD: If he was smoking, why were you punished?
KID: Because I set fire to him.

Dumb Jokes

What's the difference between putty and
porridge?
I don't know...
Well, I wouldn't let you put in my windows.

Police have searched unsuccessfully for a
criminal with a wooden leg.
Well, why don't they just use their eyes?

Did you know there's no such word as
"gullible" in the dictionary?

Knock, knock.
Who's there?
Oops.
Oops who?
Oops, wrong address.

BOY AT CIRCUS: That knife-thrower is useless. He hasn't hit the woman once.

LITTLE GIRL: You're so stupid, you should have a brain transplant.
HER BROTHER: So should you, but the brain would reject you!

Classroom Chuckles

What do you call a teacher who falls asleep in the classroom?
Nothing – you might wake them up!

TEACHER: Ravi, why did Robin Hood take from the rich?
RAVI: Because the poor didn't have anything worth robbing.

BIOLOGY TEACHER: Rebecca, where is your appendix?
REBECCA: I don't know.
BIOLOGY TEACHER: You must know!
REBECCA: No. It was removed last year, and I don't know where the surgeon put it.

TEACHER: Ryan, how many sides does the Pentagon have?
RYAN: Two. Inside and outside.

Eliza: Mrs MacTier, would you punish me for something I hadn't done?

Mrs MacTier: Of course not, Eliza.

Eliza: Good, because I haven't done my assignment.

Medical Madness

Doctor, doctor, I've only 59 seconds left to live!
Calm down, I'll be with you in a minute.

Doctor, doctor, tomatoes are growing out my ears!
Gracious. How's that happened?
No idea. I planted onions.

Doctor, doctor. I need some pills for my dreadful insomnia.
Nonsense! All you need is a good night's sleep.

PATIENT: Are bagels healthy?
DOCTOR: Well, I've never seen a sick one.

PATIENT: Doctor, doctor,
I can't control my temper.
DOCTOR: Pardon?
PATIENT: I'VE JUST TOLD YOU!!

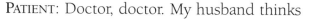

PATIENT: Doctor, doctor. My husband thinks
I'm mad!
DOCTOR: Why?
PATIENT: Because I like chocolate muffins.
DOCTOR: But I like chocolate muffins.
PATIENT: Great! You must come and see my
collection. I've got hundreds of them.

Doctor, doctor.

When I drink

a milkshake

I get a stabbing pain

in my eye.

Try taking the straw

out!

Ghoulish Giggles

What's red and looks like a monster?
A red monster.

KID CANNIBAL: I don't like the look in
Dad's eyes!
MOTHER CANNIBAL: Well just eat his fingers
then.

What do vampires become
after they are 100?
101.

Girl ghost: My Dad is 600 years
old, and hasn't got a single white
hair!

Boy ghost: How's that?

Girl ghost: He's headless.

YOUNG WOMAN: When you said our date would be a hair-raising experience, I didn't think you'd turn into a werewolf!

1ST VAMPIRE: What's the matter?
2ND VAMPIRE: Oh, that person I was chasing escaped.
1ST VAMPIRE: Don't worry. There'll be other victims to bite.
2ND VAMPIRE: No there won't. This one's got my false teeth stuck in his neck!

Insults and Grouches

HAIRDRESSER: How would you like your hair, Madam?

WOMAN: Could you cut it very short on one side, and leave it long on the other, with a crooked fringe at the front, and a big tuft on the crown?

HAIRDRESSER: Oh! I couldn't do that!

WOMAN: Why ever not? You did last time!

LITTLE BOY: I love nature!

HIS SISTER: That's very generous considering what nature's done to you.

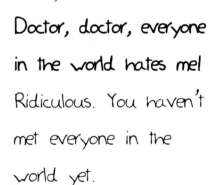

Doctor, doctor, everyone in the world hates me!

Ridiculous. You haven't met everyone in the world yet.

My boyfriend is so mean. He told me he'd bought me diamonds, and all I got was a lousy pack of cards.

My girlfriend said I looked like a million dollars.
Yeah, green and wrinkled.

I wouldn't say he was an ugly actor, but he had the perfect face for radio.

SHOP ASSISTANT: Let me straighten your gloves Madam, they look wrinkled.
CUSTOMER: But I'm not wearing any gloves!

Beastly Banter

Why did the monkey fall out of the tree?
Because it was dead.
Why did the second monkey fall out of
the tree?
Because it was hit by the first monkey.
Why did the elephant fall off her
skateboard?
Because she was hit by falling
monkeys.

What do you get if you
cross a hydraulic drill
with a kangaroo?
Big holes in the outback.

What's white
with purple feet?
A polar bear
crushing grapes.

What do you get if you cross
a gorilla with a computer?
A great big hairy, know-it-all.

Why does Mother Kangaroo
dread rainy days?
Because her children have to play inside.

Two lion-cubs were chasing their
zookeeper around a pen.
Mother lion shouted, "Stop playing with
your food!"

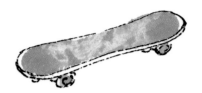

COACH: Are you any good at tennis, Dennis?
DENNIS: Yes and no.
COACH: What do you mean, "yes and no"?
DENNIS: Yes, I'm no good at tennis.

DAD: Jack, why didn't you play golf with
Lisa today?
JACK: Would you play golf with a cheat?
DAD: Definitely not!
JACK: Neither would Lisa!

COACH: Who here can jump higher than this
goal-post?
KID: I can, Coach.
COACH: But you're the worst
in the class.
KID: Maybe, but goal-posts
can't jump!

An octopus went to a shop and bought three pairs of football boots. Why did she leave two feet bare?
Well, she had to tie her laces somehow!

ANN: My dad has gold medals for golf, swimming and tennis.
DAN: Really? He must be a brilliant sportsman.
ANN: No, he's a burglar.

Fruit Funnies

What's yellow and stands in the corner?
A naughty banana.

I'm going to put this manure on my strawberries
Really? I like cream on mine.

What goes out orange and comes back white?
An orange in a snowstorm.

What's yellow

and bouncy?

A banana on a

pogo stick.

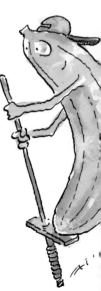

Why did the lemon
wear a blue shirt?
His red one was
in the wash.

What's the difference between an elephant
and a peach?
Don't know.
Well I'll never ask you to make fruit salad.

Why are cherries never lonely?
They always go in bunches.

Why did the pineapple
wear sunglasses on
holiday?
He didn't want to be
recognized.

What did the baby caterpillar say to his sister when he saw a butterfly?
You'll never get me up in one of those things.

CHILD: Dad, do spiders taste nice?
DAD: Why do you have to ask such revolting questions during dinner?
CHILD: Because that lettuce you just ate had a spider on it.

What do you call a man who keeps bees down his pants?
Very stupid!

What goes "99, squelch"?
A centipede with a wet shoe.

What's the difference between
slugs and snails?
Snails taste crunchier.

What pop singer do wasps prefer?
Sting.

Why do slugs wear green jackets?
So they can slide across cabbage
undetected.

What's worse than a piranha with toothache?
A centipede with athlete's foot!

Freaky Families

What do you get if you cross your kid sister with a boomerang?

A pest that you can't get rid of.

Daddy, daddy, I want to go to the zoo.
Don't worry, the zoo-keeper will round you up when she's ready.

My grandmother is amazing. She's ninety-nine and hasn't got a single white hair.
I know – she's completely bald!

LITTLE GIRL: Auntie, why are you throwing spaghetti in the fish pond?
AUNTIE: Spaghetti scares the sharks away.
LITTLE GIRL: But there aren't any sharks around here!
AUNTIE: That's because of the spaghetti.

My dad went next door to complain about their noisy party.

"Do you know I can't sleep through this infernal noise?"

"I don't," said the dude next door, plucking at his guitar, "but if you hum the intro it might jog my memory."

My brother sent his photo to the lonely hearts club. They sent it back and said they weren't that lonely! That's nothing, my sister is so ugly that she can turn milk into yoghurt just by staring at it!

LITTLE BOY: Can I come round your house to play?
LITTLE GIRL: Only if you're a good whistler.
LITTLE BOY: Why?
LITTLE GIRL: There's no lock on our bathroom door.

Alien Antics

KID ALIEN: Mother! Can you make me a sandwich?
MOTHER ALIEN: Give it a rest. I've only got eight pairs of hands.

PATIENT: Doctor, I keep thinking I'm an alien.
DOCTOR: Rubbish you just need a holiday.
PATIENT: Mmm... I've heard Saturn is very good in springtime.

Why do business-aliens put humans in their briefcases? They like to take a packed lunch to work.

SPACEMAN: Is there intelligent life on Mars?
MARTIAN: There was till you arrived.

Down at the Funny Farm

FIRST HORSE: Neigh.
SECOND HORSE: Quack.
FIRST HORSE: What do you mean, "Quack"?
SECOND HORSE: I'm learning a foreign language.

What do you give an angry bull?
Plenty of room.

What is the worst-dressed animal?
A horse – because it wears shoes without socks.

CARLOS: Where's your pig going to sleep?
MARIA: In my bedroom.
CARLOS: But what about the smell?
MARIA: Porky will get used to it.

FARMER 1: My dog is really brainy.
FARMER 2: How can you tell?
FARMER 1: Well, yesterday I asked him to subtract ten from ten and he said nothing.

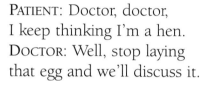

PATIENT: Doctor, doctor, I keep thinking I'm a hen.
DOCTOR: Well, stop laying that egg and we'll discuss it.

What goes, "aab, aab"?
A sheep walking backwards.
What goes, "oom, oom"?
A cow walking backwards.
No, a sheep walking backwards with an identity crisis.

DINER: How often do you wipe the tables here?!
WAITRESS: Don't know. I've only worked here a year.

DINER: Why have you served my food in a trough?
WAITRESS: Well, Chef told me you ate like a pig.

Waiter, waiter, there's only one pea in my vegetable soup!
OK. I'll cut it in two for you.

DINER: I'd like a mud sandwich, with a gherkin and mustard, served on white bread.
WAITER: Sorry, Madam, I couldn't possibly serve you that.
DINER: Why ever not?
WAITER: We've run out of gherkins.

Waiter, waiter, there's no apple in this apple pie.
So what? Ever heard of a cat in cat food?

Waiter, waiter, your tie's fallen in my soup!
Don't worry, Madam, it's dry-clean.

Waiter! This stew is like eating dog-sick!
So you often eat dog-sick do you, Sir?

Hilarious Ha-hahs!

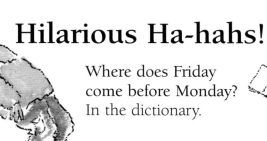

Where does Friday come before Monday? In the dictionary.

What gets smaller when you turn it upside down?
The number 9.

What do you have to break before you can use it?
An egg.

Q: Peter Piper picked a peck of pickled pepper. How many "ps" in that?
A: There aren't any "ps" in THAT!

A girl stepped into the bath without getting wet. How?
The bath was empty.

What gets nearer and nearer, but never arrives?
Tomorrow.

How many times can you subtract 10 from 100?
Once, because after that you wouldn't be subtracting from 100 anymore.

Which hand should you use to stir coffee?
Neither, you should use a spoon.

Q: Name two birds that can't fly.
A: An ostrich and a dead parrot.

Stinks!

NAOMI: I've hidden my money somewhere my brother will never find it.
BETHANY: Where?
NAOMI: Under the soap.

What's orange and smells of carrots?
Rabbit sick.

What do you give an elephant with an upset stomach?
Lots of room.

Why do giraffes have long necks? Have you ever smelt their socks?

What's green, hairy and smells?
A monster's bottom.

What did one eye say to the other eye?
Just between us, something smells.

Surgery Sillies

Doctor, every night I dream that my friends will shoot me in the back. What can I do?
Wear a bullet-proof vest?

Ah, Mr Feeble. Have those muscle-building pills done you
any good?
No, I couldn't
unscrew the bottle.

My doctor told me to take up swimming to lose weight, but I told her to forget it!
Why?
Have you ever seen a whale!

Why do surgeons wear gloves?
So if the patient dies they can't dust for fingerprints.

DOCTOR: Your cough sounds better today.
PATIENT: It should do, I've been practising all week.

Doctor, after my ingrowing toenail operation will I be able to tap dance?
Of course, Madam.
Great, because I can't tap dance now.

Hello, hello! I feel sooo... BAD! I ache all over, I've got stabbing pains in my head, a racking cough, and I can hardly move....
Are you phoning the hospital?
No. The undertaker.

Birdbrains

"Doctor, doctor, my husband thinks he's a swallow!"
"Well, bring him in immediately."
"I can't, he's flown south for the winter."

Why is the sun so far away?

So birds don't

hit their heads.

TEACHER: Why is the sky blue?
PUPIL: So birds can tell if they're flying upside down.

Why do owls fly at night?
Because they don't know how to drive.

One crow said to the other,
"Look at that jet plane. I wish
I could fly that fast!"
The other crow said,
"You could, if your bottom was
on fire."

Why do storks stand on one leg?

They'd fall over if they didn't!

Even Dumber Jokes

SHOP ASSISTANT: Buy this cleaning fluid!
It does half your housework for you.
CUSTOMER: I'll take two bottles.

MOTHER: Maria! Why are you standing in front
of the mirror with your eyes shut?
MARIA: I want to know how I look when
I'm sleeping.

A husband and wife pack their suitcases in a rush and make it to the airport just in time. "I wish I'd bought the refrigerator" said the wife. "Whatever for?" asked her husband tetchily. "Our tickets are on top of it."

Will you remember me tomorrow?
Yes.
Will you remember me in a year?
Yes.
Will you remember me in five years?
Yes.
Knock, knock.
Who's there?
Me. I thought you said
you'd remember me!

CUSTOMER: I demand a refund on this coat. It's got a waterproof label, but I got soaked in the rain.
SHOP ASSISTANT: Well, Madam, only the label says, "waterproof".

Travel Titters

On the train:
Excuse me, I think you're sitting in my seat.
I'm not. Prove it.
Well, I left my ice-cream on it....

Passenger: Can I take this train to Frankfurt?
GUARD: No, it's much too heavy.

OMAR: Dad, what was the name of the last station we stopped at?
DAD: I wasn't looking – I'm trying to do the crossword!
OMAR: OK. I just thought you might want to know where little Muhammad got off.

Doctor, doctor, I keep stealing cars.
Take these pills once a day. If they don't work,
bring me a Porsche on your next visit.

A passenger, frustrated by the slow-moving
train, shouted at the driver,
"Can't you go any quicker?"
"Yes, Sir, but I'm not supposed to leave
the train."

Doctor, doctor, my husband thinks he's a car!
This medicine should cure him.
But how will I get home?

Silly Students

TEACHER: Pedro, what was the first thing King Henry did when he came to the throne?
PEDRO: Sat down?

TEACHER: Gary! I asked you to draw your pet on the blackboard and you've done nothing!
GARY: I have – it's my black cat at night.

MUSIC TEACHER: Brad, why are you standing on your chair?
BRAD: So I can reach the top notes, Sir.

MRS PATEL: Jenny, why have you got potatoes in your ears?
JENNY: Could you speak up please, I've got potatoes in my ears.

TEACHER: Beth, can you tell me the eight times table?
BETH: If you don't know it, how should I?

Crazy Creatures

What eats cheese and says, "miaow"?
A mouse with an identity crisis.

Adam and Eve were naming the animals.
"I name that one a duck-billed platypus",
said Eve.
"Why on earth is it a duck-billed platypus?"
asked Adam.
"Because it looks like one, silly", said Eve.

How do you stop moles digging in your
garden?
Confiscate their spades.

What do you get
if you cross
a porcupine with
a giraffe?
A very long
toothbrush.

What's green
and squirts jam at you?
A frog eating a doughnut.

Did you hear about...?

Did you hear about the idiot who took a year to finish a puzzle?
He kept boasting that it said "4 to 6 years" on the box.

Did you hear about the woman who stopped playing the trumpet after three years?
She ran out of breath.

Hear about the idiot who attempted to swim the Atlantic Ocean?
Halfway across he got tired and swam back!

Did you hear about the cannibal who came back from vacation with his arms missing? He stayed in a self-catering apartment.

Did you hear about the scientist who discovered electricity? They got a nasty shock.

Did you hear about the vain actor? Whenever he heard a thunderclap in a storm, he took a bow.

Did you hear about the two eggs boiling in a saucepan? One said, "Phew, it's hot in here." The other said, "That's nothing. Next they'll crack your head open."

Gruesome Gags

CANNIBAL ONE: I don't know what to make of my husband these days.
CANNIBAL TWO: How about a stew?

LITTLE BOY: Mother, I don't want to go to school today. The other kids call me "werewolf".
MOTHER: Oh, shut up, and brush your face.

My brother's toes are so long and horny that he's worn out all his socks.

That's nothing. My brother's toenails are so long and hard that my dad uses him to rake the lawn.

Doctor, Doctor, I keep thinking I'm...
A ghost?
Yes! But how did you guess?
Oh, I knew it as soon as you walked through my wall.

MONSTER: Waiter, this is rice. I ordered maggots.

WAITER: Oh, *that* explains why that the man on the next table is vomiting.

Morris the monster-catcher was chased by a huge purple monster, ran into a wall, then passed out. When he woke up the purple monster was sitting next to him, muttering. "Thank goodness you haven't eaten me!" exclaimed Morris. "Be quiet", snapped the monster, "I'm saying grace."

Peculiar Pets

What do you get if you cross your cat with
a mouse?
A pet that chases itself.

How do you find a runaway tortoise?
Make a noise like a lettuce.

Doctor, doctor, I think I'm a hamster.

Well run round this wheel
and let me feed you
these seeds.

Will that cure me?

No, but my mother never
let me keep a hamster.

WOMAN: This soup is delicious – I'd enjoy it even more if your dog wasn't growling at me.
HER FRIEND: What do you expect – you're eating out of his bowl!

My brother does a really good cat impression.
Oh. Does he purr?
No, he eats cat food.

BOBBY: Dad, I'm going to the pet shop to buy some bird seed.
DAD: But you haven't got a bird, Bobby!
BOBBY: I know, so I'm going to grow one.

Mouldy Meals

What's the difference between cabbage and bogies?
Kids don't like eating cabbage.

KID: Auntie, this tea is disgusting.
AUNTIE: Oh, don't be so harsh! You'll be old and weak one day too.

JANE: My Dad's cooking is so bad that he burns salad.
YOLANDA: That's nothing. In our house the garbage disposal gets indigestion.

MOTHER: Take care, Johnny. Remember that most home accidents take place in the kitchen.
JOHNNY: I know. I've eaten enough of them.

KID: Grandad this onion soup is gross!
GRANDAD: But I've been making onion soup since before you were born.
KID: Maybe, but you didn't have to save some for me!

What's the difference between cat-sick and maggots?

Cat-sick spreads better on toast.